Adam Ta[...]

(il mig[...]

with best wishes from

the author

Gawain Douglas

20/1/23

Metanoia

Metanoia

Lord Gawain Douglas

Published by
Lord Gawain Douglas

Lord Gawain Douglas asserts his moral right to be
identified as the author of this work in accordance with the
Copyright, Design and Patents Act 1988

ISBN: 978-1-7396664-0-8

For Nicolette

Within the narrow circle of your arms
I found the wider world.

There is nothing new
In the words I write.
I write the same words
As other men.

Contents

Going to Ground

Hunkering down?
Hiding away?
Finding seclusion?
Retreating?
Regaining?
Recovering?

Yes

But seeking also
A place on
Which to stand, on
Which to think, on
Which to find that

Which has been lost...

An old place
The other place

Going to Ground.

1/8/19

In Vino

Look,

While this drunkenness lasts
I want to tell you what
I told you fifty years ago

It was just three words
There was a kiss
A cup of wine, and

Look,

A blink of an eye
Here we are
Again.

2/8/21

Years later

I opened the door
Cornwall came in.
It was a long way
I was living in Kent.

That's the thing about drink,
You see things suddenly,
How they came
Where they went.

I slouched upstairs then,
What's done's been sent.
What lived in Cornwall
All that time ago, came
Home last night to Kent.

Winter 2010

UTeti7h8433e2345df342wes23ws0ljk0piok-
0pf54t45pkl,.rebvvb
Quky7yytt21q

This poem was executed at random after cleaning the keys on my laptop keyboard with tissue and vinegar. It summarises the futility of human art and endeavour in the 21st century, but also achieves, by its uncalculating freshness, the beginning of something else.

2010

Was it a bottle or a poem?
(A dream, San Fran)

He grasped the bottle
The label read
This is a poem

He pulled the cork

The wine then
Held its breath
Gathered petticoats
Before proceeding.

He poured and words
Cascaded brilliantly
Nakedly
Into his mind.

He held the glass
Up to the light and
The poem showed

Vibrancy, depth
And weight
Of thought.

He sipped and
There were notes
Of ... hmm

Cinnamon
Greengage
Turkish Delight

Backstreet
Motorway
Napa
San Francisco.

He tipped his head
Opened his throat
Swallowed the worlds

The poem sank
Into his hands.

24/12/09

Goethe

Give me, as Goethe liked, three friends
A bottle each upon the table, and there,
The casement open onto the garden,
A stone to gaze upon, as daylight ends.
No conversation, just calm togetherness
Alone.

2009

*The paradox facing the modern poet is that he has to speak, not
out of silence, as previously, but out of riot. Therefore he has to
seek a new silence, deep within its absence.*

Lady of the Stones

I sit by my Madonna
She is tired
Has lost her strength
Her statue turned to stone
Real stone, no blood, no tears
But there has been no breath
Of salutation, prayers,
Feast days remembered
Pleas for chastity or
Moderation. Or an easy death.

Ah! Poor Madonna of the sea
I sit here now salvaging time
Upon a garden chair
Forgotten worshiper.
March winds touch carelessly
Your hardened face
The traffic rushes by
But all is silence here
About your shrine.

Pebbles taken from the beach
Nest round your feet, and little
Primulas attending you
Pay those respects I have
Forgotten how to say. For
Prayer like love needs work
To stay alive.

When April tints your grey with blue
Will you not turn again
In troubled times, your face
To me?

10/03/09

Happiness happens. We can arrange many things, a train journey, a vase of flowers, contentment even, misery certainly; but happiness herself will obey no summons; she comes and goes as she lists.

Blue Bird

The Jewel we search for endlessly was at that moment there, in the room. It felt like a presence, equally an absence; it was both. It was an invasion, maybe a retreat. It was the middle way. It was evening, we had been gardening, we were both tired and hungry. It was spring, the kitchen door was open, the dog was in and out, we started cooking, we had a glass of champagne. Nothing was wrong, nothing lurked behind, nothing (as far as we knew) crouched ahead. No bells rang. It was just the time, the five minutes of itself. Then we sat down and ate; then it was gone.

It happens.
Happiness happened.

3/4/09

She finally imparted to him her reverence and love for flowers.

Living and Dying – a brief guide

It would be good
To live so

Sleeping when
Tiredness comes

Rising when
Sleep goes

Eating
With the hunger

Furious
At Winter

Peaceful when
Sun lights
Your hands

Loving when
Beauty finds
Shy eyes

Dying in the
Dying hour

Good to
Pass so

So things
Are right.

Undated

The Boy Returns

January brought the boy.
I hadn't expected him then, being
Full of winter and whisky and woe.
But he brought the boy back again
Just casually, to say hello
And to remind me that
Old boys never die completely
And young lads never really grow.

21/1/10

Orders

It was clear that nothing had come
From the provinces
And below, in the far reaches
Of the valley, no engines ran.

Higher from the diffident peaks
Ensconced always in mist
No orders came.

It was difficult to proceed
Without instruction
Or knowing if the mission
Had been abandoned

Or not.

2009

Some things need a word of explaining if total mystification is not to ensue. Ron, Big Ron from Thanet, was someone I came to know walking the dog in the mornings on Walmer seafront. He'd been a boxer, a bouncer, had major heart surgery, was fond of his drink and generally got through a bottle or two of spirits the night before. His mood was often a little bleak, but on this morning in January it was more so as he had a bad cold in addition to other things. The poem is a conversation we had, with him bemoaning life in his strong East Kent accent, and me replying in my rather startled, posh one. Having got the grievances off his chest, he cheered up instantly. He was the pepper in the pot.

Winter conversation on Walmer seafront

'It's them fuckin bastard germs do you in init?'
'Yes indeed, those fucking bastard germs.'

'And them fuckin bastard dogs too'
'Yes, and er those fucking bastard dogs.'

'You'd do better wiv a fuckin bastard cat!'
'Absolutely, a fucking bastard cat.'

'But they fuckin bastard shit everywhere.'
'Yes, they do pooh around a bit.'

'Oh well, see ya mate.'
'Yes of course, er, see you...mate.'

January 2009

I desire

Oh, to be still
To be empty
Silent, silent,
Nothing,
Like a door
Like a cat
Like a wall
White by day
Dark by night.
Or like an
Afternoon.

A door people
Open or shut
A cat that sits on
A wall that stands
Naked to the wind
A room, empty
Silent, nothing.
Oh, to be still
In this way.
Here.
Soon.

13/12/10 ... revised 27/1/21

Cavern

There is a chord of Grieg's that
Tells you what I'm trying to say.
A 3rd contained, a 5th, a 7th
9th, 11th, a 13th maybe
15th, 17th, 21st, so wide
But just intervals, a sound
A cave, an echo there, a chasm
Black, profound. Mysterious steps
Leading us on downwards,
Stalactites, the slow drip of time.
The chord divides our mind
Infiltrates; it takes us
Far inside.

7/9/10

Each Man

I have held up the world also
Oh yes,

I have pushed and strained
And it has turned with my striving.

Though small and weightless
And insignificant, a grain
Or less,

I have stood and held and gained
And the world has moved.

2010

My Friend

The window is my friend
He chatters through the night
Randomly; he has no mind.

His words bring broken peace
I cannot find by day
Maybe without end.

So chatter on my friend
You have no purpose
Only talk of forests, wind.

And rattle on my friend,
Your promises are broken
Casually, but I don't mind.

A hundred years – a moment's sleep
Or sleep without end.
Your talk of mountains, cities,
Riven seas, sinks deep into my mind.

2010

Holding hands

I might have known
It was heaven, the way

The disfigured street
Reformed itself

Into a smile
The way the travellers

Passed as
Travellers should

And bicyclers went on
And up up up

By ones and twos and threes
Into the blue land

Wheels circling as they could
Across the clouds.

The way children turned
Olden ones at last

And how an old one at the kerb
Became a child again.

The sky laid down its mantle
On the sand

A mantle of itself for us
To walk upon

I might have known
It was heaven

I might have known
Holding your hand.

2011

Say your prayers

He muttered the prayers.
There was little point as
He couldn't remember them
Correctly and had never
Known what they meant
Anyway, but muttered,

Chuntered the prayers.
They were some sort of
Consolation, a small barrier
Between himself and the
Abyss that he feared, a
Comforter between his face
And something else.

He knelt clutching the bed
Climbed in and fell asleep.
Just for kneeling there
Somehow he was blessed.

31/10/11

Mr Niawag is my unidentical twin, my subconscious mentor, my backstage manager. He sees things I don't, he says things I won't, he is me and he isn't; he is my name backwards.

Mr Niawag remembers the day he was born

'I couldn't help wondering, when I was handed to my mother, has this all been some terrible mistake?'

Mr Niawag on Benches

Choosing the right bench
Said Mr Niawag gently
Can take a very long time
Almost a lifetime, or a bit more.
Take this one for instance –
We sat down – it has just
The right view doesn't it?
He was right, I hadn't noticed
Before, but yes, the perfect spot.

He grinned and his face was
Indelibly old. The sunset
Rendered it red parchment
The moon glanced down and
It was white sand, then
Grey, like November.
It contained all the faces
I had known and loved.

I love you said Mr Niawag
Because I am your father
I love you he said to me
Because I am your son.
Our gaze held like a thread then
Fell away. A bird flew south.

I called after him
Does anything remain?
But he was gone. Later
I heard an answer
Wing back to me,
'Just a bench with
A date on it, and a
Name, only a name'.

Walmer Beach 30/11/11

**Five observations, Stanza International Poetry Festival,
St Andrews, October 2011**

You're nae fuckin poet

If ye canna write a wee poem
Sitting on this bench,
A gull as witness
A girl passing,
Completely careless
In her loveliness, and
You, sitting, stone in hand
The sea ahead

Right in front, shocking
In its honesty

St Andrews sand.

Past that, the endless North,
Most patient place on earth
Most ancient

Waiting for you
To come.

If ye canna write a wee poem
In this situation
You're nae fuckin poet.

In view of this (inner) selfie
This admonition
Having sat without a plan
I took my pathway

Holding this rhyme.

Two poets talking before a 'Readaround'

I know....

If you get the weather here
It's heaven

If you get the rain, well
It's Scotland

I walked down the beach this morning
It was lovely

And last night the moon was shining
So full, so full

I've been coming here for the last five years
It's lovely

I stay with my mother in London on the way up
She's ninety now

Widowed of course
Widowed sadly

And my daughter too, she's thirty-four now
Thirty-four

Married of course
Married
Happily...

And my husband, he doesn't come with me now
Hates poetry

Thinks it's a waste of time, doesn't understand it
Sadly, sadly

I don't mind

The Georgian poet's cancelled, couldn't get through this time
Unfortunately

We'll have readaround in a minute
Be lovely ... lovely

Poetess

He held the poet's hand
Shook it briefly, felt her sand
Shift, her beach tremble
Beneath his tread, her fingers

Sticks and stones
Crow's foot bones
Inside his own

So delicate

Her pallid eye
Broke open
A dawn
A northern sky.

Boiling up

The poet frowned
His forehead heaved
Like boiling jam
He raised his pen
An eagle poised
For downward plunge
A murdered rhyme
A literary
Orgasm

Never a noise...

His eyebrows curled

Slowly

Boiling again

He wrote the date

And then...

His name.

Poets' Corner

They gathered round and looked at him, the poets. Being tired
he saw them as they were, beneath. Crows, thrushes, seagulls,
mostly birds, a sky or two, an open sea, a storm, occasional
rocks inaccessible, and shadowed hills. So beautiful
their beaches, slopes, their alien smiles.

Gently, bird like, they stared at him; they knew, he understood,
he wasn't one of them, not part of poet world, not yet.

A stork with wispy hair and spectacles and pipe stem trousered
legs, the leader of the crew, hopped near and blinked at him
with avian dispassion – on one leg stood and pecked the sky

In valediction.

He turned away, not admitted to their realm

Not yet.

Bridges

People who cross bridges
Are always free.
Look at them swinging
Their arms, faces to the wind.
You don't cross a bridge to
Get to the other side
You cross just to be there.

See, everywhere's a bridge now
Just swing your arms
Raise your face, wide to the wind.

13/3/12

Mr Niawag recognizes change
'Muss es sein?
Es muss sein.'

Mr Niawag felt very queer on Sunday night
And on Monday he couldn't go into
The kitchen

It was simmering with something...
A smell he did, but didn't recognize ... bitter
Lemons? The future?

On Tuesday it was the lounge.
They couldn't bear each other, *his* dithering
Uncertainty, *its* carpet of blue and green regrets.
Chinese.

On Wednesday the music room screamed at him to get out.
Motzarted him.
Demi-semiquavered him.

On Thursday the bedrooms locked their doors, one by one.
Do not disturb. They
Required new tenants.

On Friday his only sanctuary was the hall
He paced up and down, no shadows
Lay there, only the pooling sky.

He opened the front door smiling.
He raised two fingers at futility. On Saturday
He ate a good breakfast.

On Sunday he walked softly into the street
Wearing the moccasins of age.

He closed the door.
He didn't look back.
One never does.
On a final journey
There is no return.

3/8/12

The poet should respect what he has written; sometimes a later intended improvement is actually worse and distorts an emphasis or subtlety which the eyes of hindsight do not perceive. However sometime there is no choice but to rip it up!

Poems?

Not quite what you think
Said Mr. Niawag.
Not thoughts
Or feelings
Or words

But statues
Carved at
The beginning
By a God

Who might have
Known better.

Some dwell
In caverns
Underground

Others stand
On hillsides
Facing south.

When you want poems
Don't write or think
But go at night

Take them
While they rest
Bring them home

Sit them down
Comfort them
They are lost

They need a mind
They need a mouth

They die
Most easily.

Sometimes
they will live

Will speak.

You must hurry
Not many
Are left.

29/9/12

These poems in this book come from that division, that no man's land, existing in myself, between the spirit and the flesh.

Daffodils

We glanced at each other.

It was, you might say
A look of some caution
Been a long time, a
Long relationship. We
Need a change probably.

But, still the smile,
Grey, distracted, sunken
In my case – in yours
Yellow, fresh, delightful,
As always. You never
Seem to age. You will die
Young and I will do
The opposite, but will try to
Remember what you said.

We stood a while,
A bit awkwardly,
Not quite knowing
The correct form

Nodded briefly
At each other.

I walked into town.

Walmer, February 2013

Dentistry

Having dreaded the occasion
I realised this was
Where I should be
In dentistry.

Flat on my back, four
Hands in my mouth, the
Gentle and eternal drill
The faces loving me.

Through the skylight, the
Impossible, temporary
Clouds.

14/5/13

The Augury of the eggs

These shells are soft, too soft
They crack inside the hand.

The whites congeal into
Opacity – miasmic, dead.

The yokes lurk dully
With a lethal, amber life.

Look, here, be careful.
This morning, watch your tread

14/5/13

Cracks

Cracks in the ceiling
Cracks in the walls
Cracks in the floor
Spreading, dividing,
In, also, the teacups,
Plates, look at them
Multiplying, widening
Everywhere, leading
To that other place. But
In your face nothing
Happens. Nothing.

It is unmarked
Pristine.

Where are the cracks
In your face?

23/9/13

Tracks

++

....

++

Undated

Sand

I know those fingers
I know those hands
They are mine
They are yours
They are everyone's
They have been in every
Corner of the world
Different places, lands,
They have touched, held,
Held themselves at night
Clutched sanity at night, touched
Faces, other faces, allowed sands
To trickle from their palms.

My hands are yours, are everyone's
We are each other's hands.

5/7/14

Outside the British Library

Daffodils

How could you find your way
To the same place, in the same month
To the same doorstep, on the same day?

You promised last year when we said
Goodbye that you would come again
But I didn't believe you at all

Nor think it possible you could
Cross the ravening sea, that
Odyssey of winter one more time.

I didn't understand your utter
Faithfulness, your impossible beauty,
That your adoration of the sun triumphs
Always over everything
In endless, golden rhyme.

I am yours
I salute you
I worship you
I will not, cannot
Doubt you
Again.

13/1/15

Mr N is thoughtless

Mr Niawag had no thoughts left
Each time one came he deleted it
Replacing with a cloud
Plucked from the wind.

Sitting on his bench that
February day he had no room
For any foolishness, only
Clouds, stretching far away
Beyond his mind.

3/2/15

Mine

Give me the strength of stone
Give me the fury of the seas
The bitterness of sky
Give me my little place
Between the stars.
Give me my inheritance
Now.

Mein

Gib mir die Festigkeit von Stein
Gib mir die Wut des Meeres
Die Bitterkeit des Himmels
Gib mir mein kleines Nest
Zwischen den Sternen.
Gib mir mein Erbe
Jetzt.

29/1/16

To Volker, my German son in law

The Road

They know their spot
Exactly where they are
How they arrived
The journey here.
Look at them – poised,
Relaxed, indifferent,
Philosophers, the feet.
Chatting amongst themselves

'Ah! There's some other feet
Let's muse awhile
The trials of the way
Not far to go
Another push perhaps.'

No!
It's just that freak above
Who's so confused
The passenger, the head
Look at him, grimacing
Twisting, mouthing,
Unhappy with his lot.
He's afraid.
He knows nothing
About the road
He didn't want to come
He doesn't want to go.

28/2/16

Outfacing the Void

Now Winter's upon me
Striding towards me
Waving his arms
Shaking his fists
Shouting, laughing
Blackening sky. Now
We're best buddies
(Safer that way) now
We're together
Walking together

At least I know
The direction.
Pretences gone
Striding together now
Towards the cold
Laughing, shouting
Shaking our fists
Waving our arms
Towards the dark.

5/10/16

Passing on

Why do you think it will be different for you?
Why do you think you are a special case?
Why do you think you won't go screaming
And grovelling through that portal
Like the last man and the next?

For you my friend, no special peace,
No 'Premier' departure lounge.
For you, the packaged death of those
Good men who went before
Will do quite well enough.

The dark time of the year 2017

Tree

It had to happen
After all this time
This isolation, this
Solitude in company
This 'Selva Oscura'
This middle way
This final way.

It had to happen
That she fell in love
Not with a man or beast
Or woman, as
You might think, no!
But with a tree.

She loved a tree.

It had to happen
The call was heard
The change took place.
All is change
Said Heraclitus
Those were his words.
He knew. This change
Brought peace.

The bright time of the year 2017

Winter Light

Goodbyes may be like this
The sitting room ablaze
With winter light
The carpet radiant
With the past.
Those yellow days.

And you and I
Seated as though
Waiting for a train
Quite formally with
Hands on knees
And backs erect

Not quite relaxed.
Our eyes meet, touch, dart
Nervously around.
The mantlepiece, a stage,
Reveals the mini
Dramas of our time.

Our sitting room is
Now a place in which
We watch for something else.
The winter light
So fierce, so passionate
Is briefly ours.

2017

A Star came down to me

Mr Niawag went to the window and looked at the Plough. A star parachuted right down to the ledge and spoke to him. The conversation went something like this. 'How are you?' 'I'm sort of all right, and you?' 'I'm fine – when you're finally a star you worry less. Things stay much the same. We sleep a lot – a good night's sleep for a star's a million years – a mere blinkle. We feel the everlasting cold but stay so warm, so warm. We chat by starmail overnight and often wait ten million years for a reply – a week or so to us. 'I see' said Mr N, 'And how long does all this take, becoming a star I mean?' 'A considerable period of timelessness', said the star smiling broadly. 'But it happens in the end, if you don't interfere too much. If I were you I'd stop worrying about details and enjoy the ride. Good night.'

Slowly, but with infinite speed the star adjusted his position to 106 billion light years above Niawag's bedroom window. 'Good night' said Mr N and slept at once. He'd found the confidant he'd been looking for.

3.00 am, some night in mid-December 2017

Diversion, Ashford, Kent

That garage you passed to buy crisps in
Because you knew the man who owned it
Although you couldn't quite recall his name
And because all those years ago you taught
His daughter the piano at school.

That garage you passed to buy crisps in
Double the cost of supermarket crisps
But you bought them anyway because
They reminded you, they gave you a
Thread to that long ago bit of your life which...

Yes, that garage is now closed, bought by
BP or something.

You will not make that costly diversion anymore.
You may not, cannot go that way again.

February 2018

Baggage

The trouble's the suitcases.
Year one you pick one up
Year two, number two
Year three and four the same
Year ten, it's getting heavy
Pulling ten suitcases
Down the street all
The way to school.
Year twenty it's quite a load
Every time you walk into town
Or get onto a bus
Twenty suitcases go with you.
Year forty, you can imagine, it's
Laughable, forty of the buggers
Stretching all round the square.
No wonder your shoulders are
Bent dragging all those suitcases.
Makes people laugh.

Year sixty-eight I'm dragging
Sixty eighty-eight fucking suitcases
Onto the train and you tell me
I'm looking tired!

2018

Unison

And the thrush said
'Be still and kneel,
Collect your leaves
That I may sing
Our song'.

26/9/18

Winter Flowers

I have found the vase
Autumn is here
The time is brief
I will arrange the flowers.

Autumn 2018

Prophecy

'Library's closed' **she said.**

I'd been on the edge of something that might have been or was about to be important, when she said it, *'Library's closed'*, which was difficult to understand as people were going in and out. But that was it. Late September in the air. Earlier that afternoon walking into town, out-facing an envoy from the North, I turned back towards home when the sun began to peer. However, I chose to read the news.

'Library's closed' she said. *'I've just sat down'* I said. *'Library's closed'* she said. *'**All right**'* I said. Picking up my bag with the £1.00 salad cream and correction pen from China, from Poundland, and my whole milk and cheese slices from sad cows, from Iceland, I left the sterile airlessness of an English reading room. How right she'd been to winkle me with her forked, librarian-whetted tongue. Outside I received the warm embrace of an English summer afternoon. A final kiss. It said to me, *'Everything's ok, everything's all right. You will live a short but happy life from now. Walk on into winter'*.

'Library's closed' she'd said, but something else had opened at my feet.

Autumn 2018

Bendigo
Garden Guru

I close the window before that thing called work.
Bendigo looks up – his shrinking patch of sun.
His deep brown coat against the green and gold
Seems fragile yet enduring. Sacred tapestry,
The threads are mostly woven now. He
Knows Time's but a breath, knows peace
He feels contentment in his canine place.
This is his Eden and the Paradise he will not lose.
I, burdened with complexity, lack of simpleness
Take what I can from him.

11/11/18

Prayer is...

Standing, dawn
A doorstep
November
Nor'easter
The gate ajar.

Prayer is...

Watching later
A ripped sunrise
Sea shore, the wind,
As a die, straight
From the Urals.

Prayer is...

Spying a
Crouched moon
December 3.00 am
Holy words
finding the hands
At last, at dawn.

Prayer is...

Mouthing the hopes,
Culling the lies
Birthing the truth.
Words fall from the pen
February rain.

Prayer is...

Waiting for
Spring
Street corner.
The future – now.
Eastward, the
Egyptian light.

January 27th 2019

February

So gentle the wound
Given by a flower
A frail petal
Of bright sun.

Forgotten tears catch
An old man's throat.

13/2/19

Haikus

So I asked Basho
Where is the exit?
He pointed to the way in.

The bench on the front
Waits for someone to arrive.
Night.

My wife pauses
By the garden gate
Forgetting...

Leaving for work.
A cat on the road
Rolls happily in the sun.

Why would I cut it down?
The apple tree has green yet
On its old fingers.

February 2019

Farewell to Henry Cummings
Professor of Singing, R.A.M.
North London April 1972

It was spring in
Maida Vale, London
When we saw you
For the last time Sir.

You were old, lame,
On your doorstep,
And we were young.
You touched our baby's
Hair

Translucent, new born
And shining in
The urban spring
Surrounding us
There.

A gifted peace,
Beingness, a scarf
Of joy bound us
In the shimmering
Air.

Five decades on
The moment holds,
Time's candle gutters.
I say goodbye, once more,
Sir.

21/2/19

An Alternative View

Don't be too concerned
Nothing's wrong, curled
Up you are in bed
The year is sound
The earth is round.
Below, a wee bird
Opens its throat,
Maister Mouse peeps oot,
The worlds collide, abound.

12/3/19

A Birthday Poem for Tony and Niki
recalling an evening together

So, Time appeared
Between the cup and lip.
She grinned and said
'Where you will be
And where you are
And where you were
Is just contained
In one small sip
Of good champagne
Or Beaujolais.'

'I can be held
I may yet pause,
If I am charmed
I may relax my grip
Briefly, for just cause
As now is here.
But only when three
Gather in my name
In jollity
And bid me stay
Twixt cup and lip.'

17/3/19

A Warning from the Gods

The hand on the back of my neck
Comes from outer space
Beyond any time I know.
Its touch consoles and warns
And says, 'The hour has come
Dwell in the age you've reached
Before it is too late.
Enjoy the pleasures now
Of being old and strong.'

23/3/19

The Wayside

This place should be of interest,
It's where we fall. Look!
More pleasing than the road ahead,
So straight and grey.
Wild thyme, marjoram grow here
Upon a grassy bank.
Below, meadows, many trees
And then a stream. Listen!
Voices of women and children.
This place is named, I think,
Elysium.

27/3/19

Love Sonnet

What can I give you who have
Nothing and everything? you
Who are wiser than the moon
As foolish as that sunbeam
At your feet. You, who's talk
Is in my mouth who's thoughts
Are in my brain, who's legs walk
In my legs, who's fingers play
Piano inside my own. You,
You who have given all and
Taken everything I had,
What can I give you now?
What can we give each other
Now, as a final gift?

Undated

The Horologist

Dwelling with a hundred clocks
He found a different time.
The ticks ticked on and on
The dial hands, with Phoebus
Climbed their globes and fell again.
The hours chimed according
To their fate. But Time herself
Moved not, stayed absolutely still.

5/4/19

To Julius Pidduck, Clockmender extraordinary.

The Call

When you first call the bird
To give the bread you must,
Your voice wavers, is untrue
You cannot find the song
You cannot find the word.

Later

After many days, many days
You catch the note and your voice
Rings out. A sunbeam
Touches the bird's heart.

Later

After many years, many years
It flies onto your hand.

22/4/19

Haikus

A haiku may come
Out of complete nothingness.
Don't think about it.

Driving through a cherry storm
My heart forgets to beat.
Blossom falls, taking a life.

Summoned by the birds
Hearing sharp, the call of life
Finding his own voice.

April 2019

Facing the unknown
Its arms fallen to the earth.
The old tree. Winter.

June 2019

Drink

Of course I drink when I'm with you
Because sober, we rob each other
Of who we are, and the drink replaces it,
That theft, with who we were; leads us away
From the accusatory table and those
Staring walls, to the other side of the bottle,
Into the first glass, the whisky glass of Time.

There, the sunlight glints miraculously
Into the amber gold of spirit held,
Into the other life that
Was ours to come.

25/6/19

July Choir

The choir of Hollyhocks
Had outgrown sex.

At nine feet tall the boss
Looked down

Benevolently erect
On human frailty

Said this is how it's done

Just stand and wait and
Smile and grow

And sing.

30/7/19

Clean up

'There's so much dust everywhere'
Said God.

'I'm not having those bloody tenants again
Cancel the Global Air B and B. Now!

I give them Eden and they concrete it over
Then blow it up.'

'Bastards' he bellowed and various turrets rattled
He rather enjoyed it

'Bounders' he bellowed again and several city walls crumbled.
'You'd better be careful Lord' croaked Lucifer
Who'd been re-admitted

'Last time you did that Paradise got sucked
Into a black hole and it was the devil of a job'
(He had quite a sense of humour) 'to get us all out.'

'Scum of the earth' screamed God a third time –
He wasn't going to be dictated to by that renegade.

'I think I'll let things settle down a bit
And then start up again – go for birds and bees perhaps.'

However, there wasn't much response apart
From the statutory murmur of angelic approval
A few bells, puffs of incense and so on.

The apostles were out fishing on some celestial pond
And mother was washing pants and socks

They always looked rather nice hanging out to dry
From Heaven's high balconies.

August 2019

To David Matthews, composer

The Mask

Talking of this and that,
The political situation
Recipes (tonight's) the
Amazon – burning, burning,
All those habitations gone,
Communications, species
lost, talking of these,
Something else,
Alien, entered

His face.

Clouds

Furled, swirled
Circled his brow,

Unclouded to reveal
The mask of Zeus,
That brow, a granite cliff
Those lips, a hexagon,
Those eyes, The Milky Way
That mouth, that cavern
A river, subterranean
Underneath the sand.

A field there, of utter stillness,
Where a blackbird sings.

29/8/19

Now

The poem is not in the words

Rather in a shaft of light

Between the hibiscus and the rose

Or the old dog standing, wondering

If he's breakfasted. There's an early

Touch of autumn now

Before the heat returns.

30/8/19

Arms

And I called my father
And said three prayers
And I called my mother
And did the same

And I felt their shades
Hover close by me
And I thought of them both
And spoke their names

And the padlocked gates
Of Death were broken
And something snapped
Within my brain

And at last the dam
Of tears was sundered
And I found myself
A child again.

Ah agony! And
Each man's sorrow
To lose those friends
Those parents twain

But sorrow turns
To richer blessings
To find the road
To them again.

And I called my father
And I called my mother
And said three prayers
And spoke their names

And I felt in the night
Their arms surround me
And I knew them both
And was whole again.

Summer 2020

Route 2020

The new reality
Is difficult, has
Traps for the
Unwise, having
Sharp edges, no
Smooth corners which
To cycle round.

No, do not relax, you
May never relax now.
In this place

The road is only
Straight ahead and
Where you came from.
No byways
No left or right.

Steel glistens in
The cobalt blue.
There is iron
Under foot.

6/12/20

Poor fare

By the sheer number of times
He put the point of the pen
Onto the page, you might
Have thought something
Was cooking poetically,
A canapé, a soup, a fowl,
A savory, a Chambertin?

Mais non!
It was just porridge
With neither salt, nor milk,
Nor honey, to assuage

The sorrows
Found therein.

28/12/20

War

What can you say about March
Except the God rough handles you
From sleep, grabs you by the scruff
Shakes you till your teeth
Grind in his storm.

He rattles you round the house
He boots you out of doors
He hurls you down the road
He bellows at your back

This

'I cannot stand time wasters
Tiredness, fragility, indifference

PAH!

I will whip you
Raging and screaming
Raving and warring
Into my harbour
That is spring.'

29/12/20

On

If
It were a race Ma'am
They'd be cheering us
Round every corner
Of the track, waving
Us on, those at the front,
Those at the back.

'Come on guys,
Come on
Nearly home now
Nearly home.'

But
All that's gone, just you
And me, I think, remain.
There were others. We
Stagger in the dark Ma'am
Blindly, foolishly,
Incompetently on.

We know nought of
Who we are, or
Why, or whence
We came.

Beyond
The silence, the
Blackness ahead
There is a slippage,
The clear, distinct
Sound of
A crack.

31/12/20

Spring

Waiting in the porch
January the 27th
The very first signs.

27/1/21

And then

Afterwards
Afterwards, the
Blackbird sang a
Sweet roulade, rills burst
The garden ground, flowed on
Directly to the Amazon.
We took a bus and rowed, so fiercely,
Wildly down the star shot canyons, through
Tides of crocodiles, rhinoceros, constrictors, 'til
At last we found the setting sun – a still,
So silent pool, forgotten heart
Of Welsh oak where the blackbird
Has his dreamtime home.
He sang an upbeat trill
Of welcoming, for
Love's the passport
To the other place
We knew. Once
Long ago.

January 2021

And

Today   there was change

It had to come

                   Unexpected

Round the square

He met it   Head on

Inevitable

Endless

Stretching ever so far

Around, beyond, behind, in front

Away

Change.

After heat comes cold
          after war, peace
               after death, life
                    after noise…

He stopped   There it was

Silence.

27/1/21

Doctor, Doctor

'What would be the likelihood…?'
He tried to formulate…
'In your opinion, what are
The chances of…?'

No, he must be more direct
He watched the doctor's tie
Grey like a headstone…
'Doctor' at last, 'How long
DO I HAVE LEFT?'

The question floated like a
Feather to the floor
They watched it settle there
The medic and his charge.

The doctor smiled
And pulled his ear
And then his nose
(Always a bad sign)
He laid his hands
Upon the desk like
Steel on silk.

'No time at all' he smiled
'No time at all ha-ha
Because you see',
Leaning forward
Professionally,

'You are already dead
You know, long dead
Long gone.'

2/11/18 revised March 2021

Rain

There was a long silence and then I asked (while rain splattered the marble courtyard endlessly, evenly, caressingly in the afternoon) and then I asked *'Where is innocence, after all that's been and done?'* Mr Niawag who had been waiting for the question (while curtains of rain swept without sound the garden path, displacing, oh displacing Time to a foreign balcony) didn't hesitate for a moment. *'I'll show you'* he said and took my hand. We walked along the beach (rain flattening the grey lips of the sea to make them smile) then stopped. *'There'* said Mr N, *'There'* he said again and pointed at my feet. A white stone lay between, a seagull flew above. It circled thrice. *'There it's always been. Your life lies at your feet. It is not possible'* he said, *'you cannot kill'* he said, *'your innocence'* (while clouds tumbled down Olympian ways and rain day-tripped delightedly to France).

March 2021

Silent Shout

Now I'll show you
Shout the Hollyhocks

Talk about beauty
What do you know?

Stare at us

Watch us wave
Watch us dance

Long for our brevity
And our release.

20/7/21

Metanoia

Let your shadows,
Grey robes,
Fall from you.
They will, if you
Unclasp them,
Tumble and
Lie, rainbows
At your feet.

20/7/21

On our kitchen wall, by the sink, close to a window looking onto our small urban garden, there hangs a picture of a street in Blakeney in Norfolk. This sunlit street looks down past a hostelry on the right and two or three residents chatting on a bench on the left, to a winding river through the marshes and then out to sea. The painting is by Jason Partner. My sister Yoskyl who lived in Norfolk owned the picture, and whenever I visited her I would look at it with absorption and longing. I loved Blakeney and the view and I loved the picture which suggested to me, I suppose, a sentiment something akin to Tennyson's 'Crossing the bar'. But there was something else in the lumber room of my mind, some hint of memory or phantasy or instinct. My sister left the painting to me and when she died in 2018 it was given to me. Daily, I looked at the picture and the feelings deepened. And then it clicked – Blakeney was the gate into Dogger land.

Dogger Land, an area connecting our Eastern coast to the Netherlands, the western coasts of Germany and the Jutland Peninsula, was submerged around 6500 BC and had been a rich habitat with prehistoric animals and human habitation. Instead of the North Sea, there was a series of gently sloping hills, marsh, heavily wooded valleys, and swampy lagoons. Doggerland. Eden. Eden on our doorstep. Nice to think it was so close.

Perhaps far inside the caverns of our collective mind there is the faintest trace, an echo of tundra, forest, weald and lake, a wisp of flaxen memory of this place. **'Metanoia'** ends with this dream ground in my poem 'Blakeney'.

Blakeney

The town reverts to what it was, what it wasn't, empty space,
A lea, sky, shore, a path beyond the shore, leading
Endlessly ahead, north, dark, lake, forest, Dogger Land,
An old place, that other place.

Look in the picture on your kitchen wall
A seaside town in Norfolk, the street
Gazing northward, quietly across the marsh
Towards the horizon...

And we, you and I, revert to what we were once,
An eyelash, a glance, a strand of hair, two solitary children,
An open marsh, wending long ahead; we go
Where we must, to find forest, lake, dark, safety,
Where we have been before, long ago, the other land,
The hidden place.

Overpainted, this town. Beyond
The bright veneer, a dark horizon
Flatlined in our minds, fenland
Forest, weald, haven, now submerged
Remembered in our feet, we used to know.
Children. The Dogger Place...

FINIS August 2021

With grateful thanks to Volker Schottdorf, my son-in-law, for his invaluable help with the editing of this book and for his Photography.

Poetry runs through the generations of the ancient Douglas line. First there was Gavin Douglas, a sixteenth-century bishop and one of Scotland's most famous Renaissance characters and poets, and then William Douglas, who wrote the words for the song 'Annie Lawrie'. Gawain's father was a famous reciter of Shakespeare's sonnets, and his great-uncle, Lord Alfred Douglas, was recognized by Oscar Wilde and George Bernard Shaw as one of England's outstanding poets.